PIGEONS • PENGUINS POST TURTLES

And Other Lousy Managers

Wesley Miller

Copyeditor:
Walt Washburn (Washburn Project Management Group, LLC)
www.washburn-pmg.com
Reginald Harvey (RHA|PE – A Process Ennoblement Company)
http://www.processennoblement.com

Cover and interior illustrations:
Jeffrey Miranda (Allen, TX)
jeffmiranda2000@yahoo.com

Library of Congress Cataloguing-in-Publications Data
Library of Congress Control Number: 2011918211
Wesley Miller wesleym@yahoo.com
Pigeons • Penguins • Post Turtles (And Other Lousy Managers)
ISBN: 13: 978146678851
ISBN: 10: 146678854

To Meagan, Caitlin, Alaine, Gillian—
the greatest children that God has loaned out

To Coach Chadwick & Mrs. Higginbotham—
thanks for believing in me

To my wonderful wife, Susie

Foreword

As a youth in the late 1950s and early 1960s, I was mentored in the principles of hard work and performance excellence (*"do it right the first time"*). I *understood* that applying these concepts would result in magnificent rewards for stellar performance. Sweat equity, logic, personal integrity and an on-going quest for knowledge were the cornerstones upon which I would build the foundation of my adult experience and professional career. I *knew* that by abiding by these precepts I would achieve the success accorded to those who merited it. As a young adult in the early 1970s and 1980s it was *inconceivable* that our society would produce iconic catastrophes such as Enron, WorldCom, Arthur Andersen, Goldman Sachs, or a Bernie Madoff – just to name a few.

Little did I know my professional life would be ruled by the adolescent ideals of "managers" whose stunted emotional growth had remained trapped in the hallways and pep rallies of high school memories! How sad that for so many in our society, their high school triumphs in varsity sports or angst over not being popular would overshadow their adult experience and marginalize their adult accomplishments.

Reflecting on my own high school experience, one of the most notable memories is having been assigned to read *The Peter Principle* (1969: Peter, Laurence J. & Hull, Raymond) for an English Literature class taught by a returning special forces Vietnam veteran. That trip down memory lane made me realize the nightmares from my professional career were not merely bad dreams – they were REAL!! And the caricatures and challenges explored within the pages of _The Peter Principle_ had sprung to life from the book's pages. They were embodied in the forms of the middle managers and upper-level executives for whom I had worked!

Now forty-plus years later, I've been introduced to _Pigeons • Penguins • Post Turtles_, which for me is the missing bookend to that high school English class. At last, my corporate nightmare has been given dimension and form. Thanks is due author Wesley Miller for naming my workplace demons, and for recognizing my personal pain. My destructive encounters with **Prom Queens, Post Turtles, Pigeons, Chameleons** and **Bar Managers** among the other cast of characters are no longer unconstructive recollections that haunt me. Rather, I now have the constructs to understand better anxieties and defensive behavioral strategies that have passed for workplace politics – and I can let go of those nightmarish encounters. With each read I learn a little more about my work experience, and I celebrate the miracle of my personal survival. Even more valuable is realizing I'm better equipped to steer away from becoming one of Miller's characterizations as I move forward into roles of discretionary authority.

I wish I could have had the benefit of _Pigeons • Penguins • Post Turtles_ a few decades ago, but I probably wouldn't have been able to appreciate the insights it holds any better than I appreciated _The Peter Principle_ on my first read. Today, I'm grateful – ever so grateful – that I have read them both.

Reginald Harvey

Reggie Harvey & Associates
Process Ennoblement, Inc.
http://www.processennoblement.com

Acknowledgements

This book could not have been accomplished without the help of many friends who contributed to its success. The stories included are both fictional and nonfictional in nature, and are a collection of experiences of those who worked with me to assemble this material. I would like to thank Padmavathi Min, Reginald Harvey, Mark Herndon, Sherry Steele and John Jackola for their tireless efforts in providing me with their insights, observations, and short stories, but mainly for being my friends. I am not the best writer in the world, so to even consider this effort; I had to know that someone with a strong literary background would be my editor-in-chief. "Sir Walter Raleigh" Washburn has been filling this role for some ten years now, and I will be forever grateful for his patience and honesty, and for the encouragement that led me to undertake this book.

My children have helped shape this work by reflecting my thoughts back to me in their actions. They have challenged me by pointing out that I am "that" person I was describing (and criticizing) last week. We would argue, and then I would have to concede they were correct. Thank you, Meagan, Caitlin, Alaine, and Gillian. Thanks for making your dad insane, and for causing his hair loss, but most of all, for shaping his life in a truly meaningful way.

I would also like to thank my mother for providing inspiration, stability, and vision in my life. My mother grew up in England, which provided her with different perspectives on people than I got growing up in southeast Texas during the '60s. My mom had a saying that has stuck with me to this day, "Everyone is equal until *they* choose to lower themselves."

I played sports throughout my youth, and my many coaches through the years played heavily into my life's experiences. In Little League, I was an all-star with visions of playing professionally in the majors (MLB).[1] It was when I was going through a tough transition from Little League to working toward my big league goals that I can remember Coach Paulus' comments having a profound effect on me. He asked me a simple question, "Do you know the difference between a professional and an amateur?" Being a know-it-all, I proceeded to fill the air with noise. He was shaking his head, so I finally stopped and waited for the response. He said, "An amateur practices until he gets it right; a professional practices until he can't get it wrong." [2]

Last but not least, thank you to my wife, Suzanne. Thanks for the constant correction and for trying to instill in me the English skills that I should have learned in high school. Thanks, also, for instilling in our children the need to write and explore their imaginations. Your love has helped me make it this far, and I know it will carry me through the rest of my life.

If there is anything that I would tell my readers of high school age, it is this—go to class and learn how to write!

Table Of Contents

Middle Management Abandoning Ship

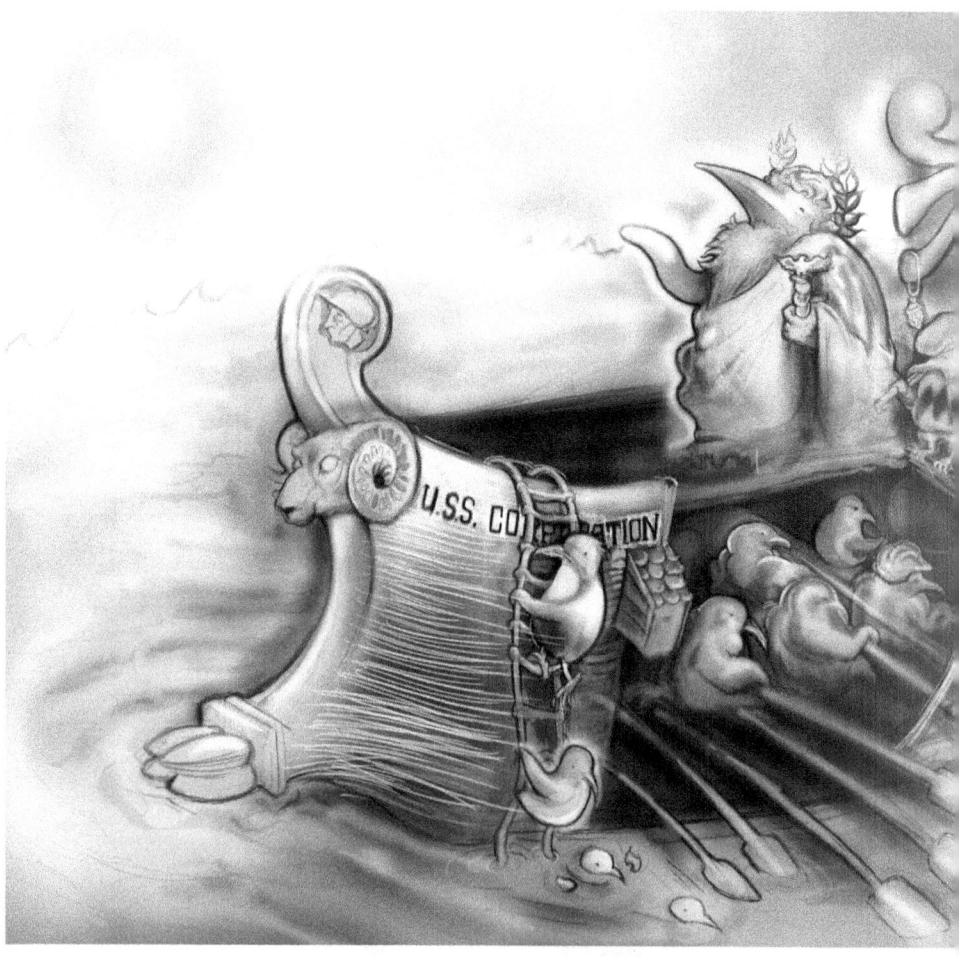

Introduction

In the late '70s a movement began to remove middle management from the ranks of corporate America, and it is still affecting corporations some forty years after that wave washed up on the executive beach. Corporations did not understand what these individuals provided. They only saw them as a cost they could do without—these well-seasoned, gentle-tempered people whom everyone so conveniently forgot were the bridge between individual contributors and top management.

Other contributing forces to the decline in middle management include the rise of the political correctness movement and the cable news media police, both of which enforce filtered views of the world within corporate America. I label the mainstream management styles that were in vogue before the '80s as *Old School* in this book. Typically confined to the Northeast and still active, Old School management is beginning to diminish as the quality of the leadership from other regions of the country becomes better known. I also define and describe several other management styles: as *Societal* (think political correctness), *New Wave* (think new math of the '80s), and *Sustainable* (think *Good to Great* from Jim Collins)[4] —a book that headlines the only management style I consider successful. In the last forty years, we have allowed Societal and New Wave thinking to dominate the landscape, impairing and disabling American corporations from reigning supreme, as they did before the '90s, thus shaping several of these management paradigms. The new buzzword these days from the political correctness crowd is *diversity*. If corporate America fails to promote managers who are qualified first and foremost, they will never move from good to great.

Social promotions overtook merit-based promotions in our school systems and eventually bled into corporate America. I can remember the first time I encountered individuals who had been held back in school. These people weren't bitter and didn't blame the teachers, the principal, or their parents; they blamed themselves for lack of effort. Something else I remember is that I never encountered a person who had been held back twice. Wonder why? In the '80s societal changes crept in, and soon social promotion became the norm. Soon teachers that believed in the social promotion idea flooded our schools.

Teachers are like managers; some are good and some are not. My in-laws are all teachers in various fields. My sister is also a teacher. My father-in-law, Charles Roberts, once told me that you can learn more from a bad teacher than a good one. Perplexed, I asked him for more insight. He went on to tell me the bad teacher (manager) exhibits habits that you do not want to mirror, and you say to yourself, "I will never be like that." The bad teacher's habits are the ones that you talk about with your coworkers, your wife, your kids, and your friends. Good teachers (or managers) do what you expect of them; however, both styles will stick in your mind and be remembered for years. (In the great USA, teaching is one of the lowest paid professions, yet teachers have the greatest impact in shaping not only the future leaders but America itself. As a nation, we need to wake up to that fact. I am not talking about college professors; rather, I am talking about those teachers who, in our formative years, ingrain in us some basis for our future direction.)

There is a philosophy quiz that gets to the core of what makes great managers/leaders. The philosophy quiz asks several questions, and I want you to read them and see how you do:

1. Name the five wealthiest people in the world.
2. Name the last five Heisman trophy winners.
3. Name the last five winners of the Miss America pageant.
4. Name ten people who have won the Nobel or Pulitzer Prize.
5. Name the last six Academy Award winners for best actor and actress.
6. Name the last decade's World Series winners.

If you are like most of us and are not a trivia buff, you answered only a few of the questions. Headlines fade rapidly into the sunset; the honors are all packed inside boxes in our attics. Now take the following quiz:

1. List a few teachers who aided your journey through school.
2. Name three friends who have helped you through a difficult time.
3. Name five people who have taught you something worthwhile.
4. Think of a few people who have made you feel appreciated and special.
5. Think of five people you enjoy spending time with.

Here, your answers probably flowed readily from your lips, as you remember those who helped you along. The point I am trying to make is that most of us do not remember the headlines of yesterday, but we do remember the people who helped define our perceptions and perspectives, who helped us form the lens we now use to view ourselves and others.

Many companies have good leaders and good managers. This is not enough. Great leaders aren't necessarily great managers; however, your great leaders should always be in senior management if your company wants to move from good to great. Most of the management styles mentioned in this book (see **Figure-1: Management Style Map**) are detrimental (per the "traits" listed in the circles) to solid growth and prosperity. To regain its interdisciplinary[5] leadership role among world economies, America will have to remove these management styles and adopt sustainable options or continue to suffer the malaise that hovers over corporate America.

I hope the book will be informative and will generate its fair share of chuckles but that it will also cause leadership to reflect upon the various management styles presented and invoke change within their organizations where it's needed.

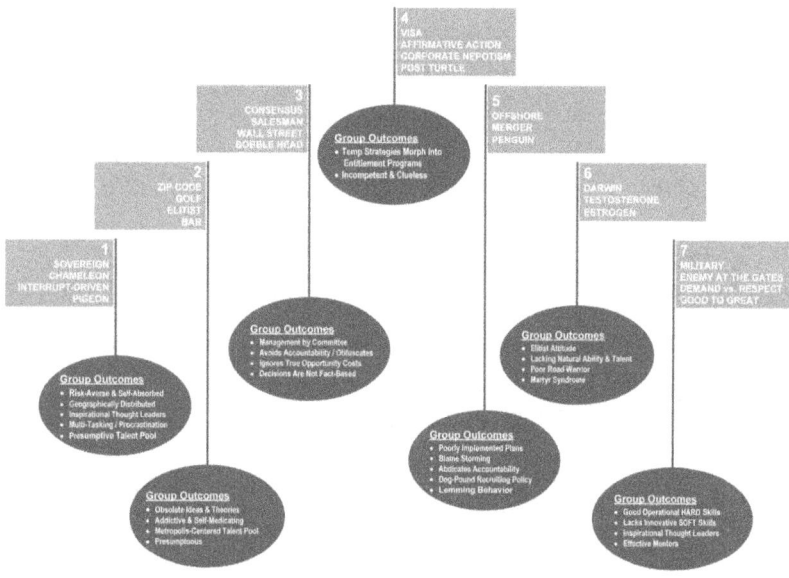

Figure-1: Management Style Map

Group No. 1

Management Styles

SOVEREIGN

CHAMELEON

INTERRUPTION-DRIVEN

PIGEON

GROUP OUTCOMES

- Risk-Averse & Self-Absorbed
- Geographically Distributed
- Inspirational Thought Leaders
- Multi-Tasking / Procrastination
- Presumptive Talent Pool

Sovereign Management

Sovereign Management

The sovereign manager provides one of the most dangerous forms of management and also one of the most damaging. These managers have a worship expectation like that of a Roman emperor. They are the epitome of hubris. They will marshal all resources at their command to move their agenda forward. If dissension among the rank and file appears, these same resources are used to quell a rebellion. A sovereign manager will use personal attacks to constantly remind you that as an individual contributor you are not capable of success. The sovereign manager builds a mentality of dependency among his troops, always keeping a leery eye out for high achievers. Once high achievers are identified, the sovereign manager will move these people into non-managerial roles or onto special projects out of the limelight. The only glory to be attained is that which is reflected off of the sovereign manager. Ownership and accountability sans empowerment belong to the workforce. This equates to all of the work and blame and none of the rewards or respect. Attention from those higher in the organization for work well done is diverted back to the sovereign manager. Sovereign managers are addicted to power and will try to remain in power at all costs. You may be able to curry favor with a sovereign manager, but it will never get you higher in the organization than they are, and will most likely gain you the resentment of your peers. I worked for such a manager, and after he left several of us observed that it took the corporation almost four years to recover from his placement of people and resources. In doing so, the company let go some twenty-two individuals who had been promoted by this manager.

An example of this at the national level is watching what happens when control of Congress flips between political parties. Once in power a political party will push its agenda through, at times ignoring the legitimate, competing concerns among the American people. The future will be the judge of such actions, but it illustrates the my-way-or-the-highway mentality.

RECOMMENDATION

Senior management will need to address this at the outset because of the human resource issues arising from the demoralizing and insidious actions of sovereign managers if they are left unchecked. A broad sweeping management change is necessary that leaves no remnant behind.

Chameleon Management

Chameleon Management

The "chameleon" manager tries to be all things to some people. As a subordinate, don't expect to get attention or guidance because the chameleon only manages up. He adapts mannerisms, language, and leadership objectives consistent with whichever senior executive is within earshot. To the unsuspecting subordinate, the sudden changes in direction and "guidance" coming out of the mouth of his chameleon manager can be disorienting. However, the truth of the matter is that there is no direction or objective for the team, only one for the chameleon— who is too busily currying favor with all in power in a desperate effort to get promoted.

Once you catch on that your boss is one of these chameleons, don't waste time with frustration. Keep your eyes peeled for the closest executive, and try to anticipate how your chameleon boss will pivot so you can be there ahead of time to serve up opportunities for your boss to shine. At worst, you will help this problem boss get promoted and become another team's burden.

Chameleons most often self-destruct. They make too many mutually exclusive promises, or they find themselves in the same room with competing executives (a joy to watch—kind of like putting a chameleon on a swatch of tartan). Savvy executives will quickly understand and are perceptive to the venality. In any case, don't try to help the chameleon flame out. He will pull you into his mess without a shred of remorse, and further, will concoct a story putting you at the center of blame. Let him destroy himself on his own; it usually doesn't take too long.

RECOMMENDATION

Recognize the chameleon for who (and what) he is. Try to stay one step ahead so you can support the position of the day, and assure he has all the rope he needs. These managers are shallow. The executives with whom they vainly try to curry favor usually became executives because they could read people well. Do *your* job well so when the inevitable happens, you are not considered part of the problem.

Interruption-Driven
Management

It started with call waiting in the '70s, extended to cellular phones in the '80s, and expanded in the '90s through today with the "*i*Generation"[6] —I'm talking about the creation of the "interruption-driven" society. When I was in school, I was considered an "active" child, but when tasked with work I could stay on task and complete the work assigned to me. When my teacher complained to my mom that I had disrupted class, my mom said, "Give him more work to do," and the teacher did. Thanks, Mom. I managed to turn out fine (don't ask my wife though) despite having no prescription medication. Over the decades, we have built a myriad of interruptions into our daily lives, and we wonder why our children are on Ritalin, and other drugs I can't name, designed to calm them down. Imagine a management style that is interruption-driven. Now imagine the productivity of a company managed that way.

There are several "communication tools" that support the interruption-driven manager. It starts with e-mail, moves on to texting and instant messaging, and ends with the cadre of distractions that stem from social networking and media sites.

The premier interruption-driver and the worst and most ineffective means of corporate communication is e-mail. Yet most of corporate America still uses it. It seems as if more time is wasted checking e-mail than is wasted by smoking, taking coffee breaks, or engaging in employee celebrations. Corporate America's budgets for e-mail storage rivals most third-world countries' GDP.[7] Recently, an employee of a start-up company complained that the company had not progressed in seven months due to the staff languishing in cyberspace. He had indicated that it takes hours, if not days, for senior management to respond to e-mails. I then asked, "Why not call them?" He acted surprised saying that e-mail was his preferred way to communicate; phone calls were so old school. To make a long story short, the company folded a year later, and he was looking for a job…by calling recruiters.

The second interruption-driven driver is associated with handheld mobile devices that are used for text messaging or instant messaging (IM). The constant ping caused by the delivery of a text message drives people crazy and also has them responding reflexively. Text messaging interrupts meetings, and has started a new variant of interruption-driven management. It is ironic that "Service Level Managers" (SLM), who demand immediate answers to the questions posed in text messages sent to their teams tend to assure these teams achieve lower productivity due to the constant interruption of the text messages.

The next few interruption-driven mechanisms are associated with i-tool devices like the iPad®[8]and iPod®, and especially the iPhone®[9] (the Droid™ deserves an honorable mention). [10] These devices cause interruptions because they can provide us twenty-four-hour access to our favorite websites (examples: LinkedIn, Yahoo, and Facebook[11]), sports games and tournaments (examples: NFL and March Madness®)[12], and so forth. There are commercials for these devices showing endless ways to interrupt any occasion in which you're supposed to be participating. They divert your full attention to the cyber-device in your possession instead of permitting you to engage in the activity for which you have allotted your time. This type of mental straining spills over into work. Many companies are beginning to prohibit Facebook access during work hours, but the ever-clever employee has his device in hand while slaving away on company time.

Another internet-driven management activity is not a physical device, but the language that has developed from devices to speed up and supposedly shorten the interruption. (see **Figure-2: Periodic Text Message Table**).[13] This lexicon is known to all people under twenty-five and some even older. Most people know that "LOL" stands for "Laughing Out Loud" but can't tell you the name of the vice president of the United States.

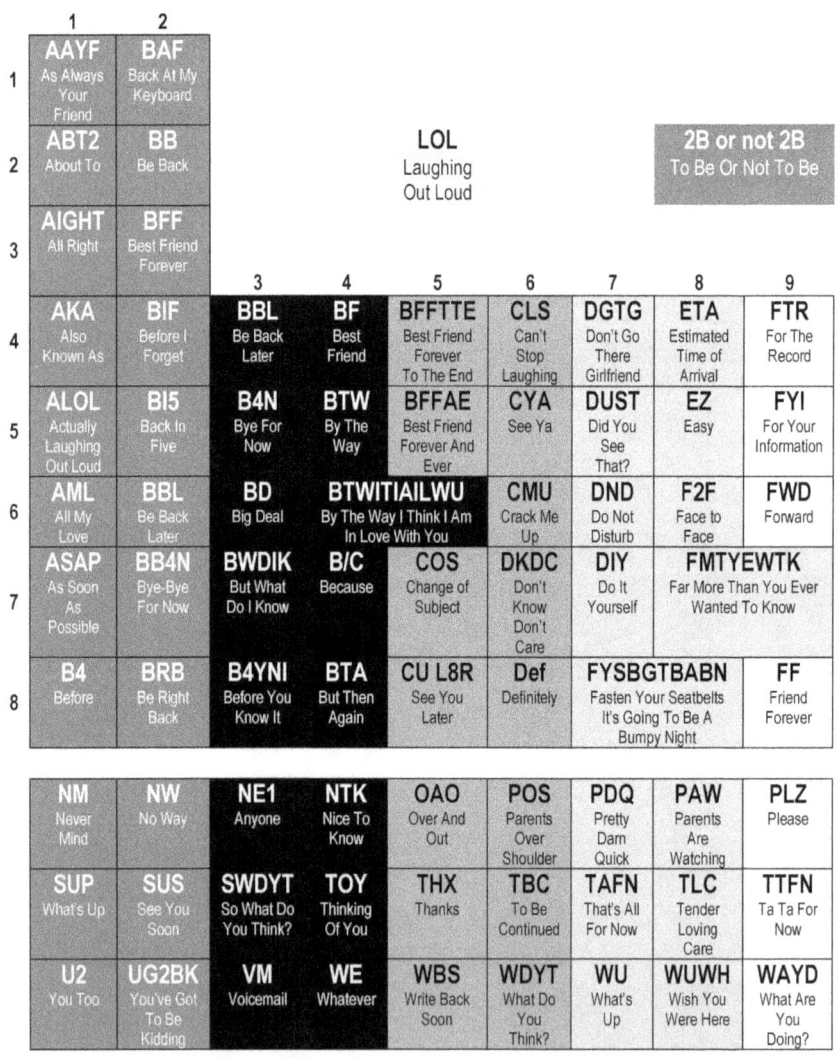

Figure-2: Periodic Text Message Table

			13	14	15	16
						LYLAB Love You Like A Brother
			HIG How's It Going?	**IDK** I Don't Know	**K** OK	**LBRG8R** Later Gator
			HO Hold On	**IYD** In Your Dreams	**KK** OK	**MYOB** Mind Your Own Business
10	**11**	**12**				
FOAF Friend OF A Friend	**G2G** Got To Go	**GOI** Get Over It	**HB** Hurry Back	**ILU** As Always Your Friend	**KMP** Keep Me Posted	**MIA** Missing In Action
FAWC For Anyone Who Cares	**GG** Gotta Go	**Grats** Congratulations	**IDC** I Don't Care	**IDGI** I Don't Get It	**LYLAS** Love You Like A Sister	**MLAS** My Lips Are Sealed
GF Girlfriend	**GRRRR** Growling	**GFI** Go For It	**ILY** I Love You	**IM** Internet Messaging	**LYL** Love You Lots	**NBD** No Big Deal
GTG Good To Know	**GL** Good Luck	**GR8** Great	**IDM** It Doesn't Matter	**JW** Just Wondering	**LOL** Laughing Out Loud	**NM** Never Mind Nice Move
GNBLFY Got Nothing But Love For You		**HSIK** How Should I Know	**JK** Just Kidding	**JP** Just Playing	**LMK** Let Me Know	**NMP** Not My Problem

Tmoro Tomorrow **2nite** Tonight

QT Cutie	**QFT** Quality Friend Time	**RUT** Are You There?	**RU** Are You?	**RBAU** Right Back At You	**Sk8r** Skater	**SLAP** Sounds Like A Plan
TFLMS Thanks For Letting Me Share	**TTG** Time To Go	**TBH** To Be Honest	**TTYL** Talk To You Later	**TMI** Too Much Information	**TY** Thank You	**U** You
WITW What In The World?	**WFM** Works For Me	**XOXO** Hugs and Kisses	**YA** Yeah	**ZZZ** Totally Bored		

The last driver for interruption-driven management is a combination of bits and pieces of the mechanisms mentioned above. The best way to describe it at this time is to use AT&T's U-Verse® digital service, the *u* in this alphabet soup. U-Verse® combines TV, radio, *i*Tunes, game applications (you name it), and can stream each to your portable device. There is more computing power in these portable devices than in the spacecraft that took men to the moon. These devices only add arrows to the quiver of the internet-driven manager, providing them with more ways to interrupt their day.

Instant messaging gives this manager unlimited opportunity to disrupt employees daily. If you do not respond within the time frame of the *unpublished* service level agreement (SLA), they are at your door demanding to know why you are not answering. This manager even goes so far as to contact you on your days off for information he could have gotten from you before you left work. Another way the interruption-driven manager wreaks havoc is to conduct unscheduled meetings, regardless of what commitments you may have confirmed and demands that you adjust your whole schedule to meet his or hers.

I know many people are saying, "What about the two-way pager or personal digital assistant (PDA)?" Perhaps they do deserve honorable mention. But either way, the cyber space- warp developed by our technology geniuses is consuming corporate America. These "communication tools" have led to an environment of constant distraction that hurts the bottom line of the company, and is disruptive to employees' personal lives as well.

RECOMMENDATION

You must put parameters and guidelines in place that identify and remove these managers. Also, the workplace must have parameters that help employees be attentive and happy at work. I have included a link[14] that shows what one employer did to help with this management style. The bottom line is you as a manager must be cognizant of your employees' time and limit interruptions.

Pigeon Management

Pigeon managers are geographically located in different regions of the country, and often a different time zone, from those they manage. This manager believes she must travel to stay in touch with her troops, because the "pigeon" manager does not have the skill set to manage remotely. Don't confuse these site meetings as a means to offer periodic and planned face-to-face time between contributors and supervisors. Though human interaction, aka "water cooler time," is vital to any leader's success, this is not the intent of the pigeon manager. What I am referring to here is the inability of a leader to skillfully build the team's confidence and sense of worth by remotely supporting their efforts.

Pigeon managers believe that face-to-face time is a means to nurture, support, and give direction to a team. They are correct in this belief, yet usually they don't succeed. The problem is the manager sees her visits as an inconvenience—time away from her family and/or personal activities. These trips are a disruption to life. Like a pigeon, this manager flies in and soils on everyone and everything before flying out the next day. Her visits are short (accomplishing little), and the team's confidence takes a hit on each visit. The team dreads all future visits from this manager and spends an inordinate amount of time and resources prepping slide shows and reports for these visits. The cleanup after these "progress update meetings" takes its toll every time, and soon resentment becomes apparent.

An easy identification point for this management type is giving low marks to remote groups and high marks to local groups. Pigeon managers may even make the remote groups report to a peer who is located at the same facility as they are, but they, too, are usually incapable of managing remotely. At this point, the manager and subordinate form a pity pool, and misery does love company. In this alliance each will defend the other. Usually it is the remote team who is viewed as the non-performers, and their inefficiency is not recognized as a result of ineffectiveness of the pigeon manager's or the subordinate's management skills.

RECOMMENDATION

Shoot the bird and appoint an on-site support manager. Invest in teleconferencing or rent a location that has teleconferencing capabilities. The on-site manager could be from another group and not necessarily of the same discipline as the group(s) he or she manages. Quite possibly, this newly appointed on-site manager will build a lasting cross-disciplinary relationship and, probably, help the organization to mature. The on-site manager is more likely to be committed to the needs of the team and have immediate access to take a pulse of the situations at the site that are detrimental to the team's effectiveness. They will be better able to marshal the teams efforts on a day-to-day basis, as the resources within the team are needed for projects that support the facility as well as the projects that are of interest to the remote manager. The on-site manager will need a strong mentor, one seasoned with managing remotely. Finally, hire a local consulting firm to provide one-on-one guidance.

Group No. 2

Management Styles

ZIP CODE

GOLF

ELITIST

BAR

GROUP OUTCOMES

- Obsolete Ideas & Theories
- Addictive & Self-Medicating
- Metropolis-Centered Talent Pool
- Presumptuous Attitude

Zip Code Management

"Zip code" management is a long-standing, Old School management style that is predominantly northeastern in nature. It encompasses cities that were major players in the industrial revolution, starting in the Midwest cities like Chicago, then moving eastward through Virginia before heading due north— finally landing in Maine. The theory behind this management style is that intelligence, and thus management ability, is contained wholly within certain zip codes that are defined by cities or between short-haul business transit corridors, most notably: New York and Boston, New York and Chicago, New York and its select suburbs, or Boston and its suburbs. Managers in these regions or transit corridors tend to appoint other managers who live in those zip codes usually by personal reference without a shred of interview evidence to support their decisions. These zip codes form the genesis of a world we will call "Shangri-la ZC." Everyone else lives in a "Boondocks ZC." This management style has many flavors:

- One is to hire a Shangri-la ZC manager from outside the company to manage a team in Boondocks ZC. This Boondocks ZC team is already performing well, but they can't be recognized until a Shangri-la ZC manager says so!
- The myth behind Shangri-la ZC management is fading, and any lingering suspicions in this management system have been rendered obsolete as teleconferencing, WebEx,[15] and video conferencing give Boondocks ZC teams representation

without having to be in a Shangri-la ZC, and they can now prove to senior management that intelligent life exists outside of the Shangri-la ZC.

An interesting aspect of this management style is revealed when a company acquires another company outside of the Shangri-la ZC, and asks (demands) individuals from Boondocks ZC to move to Shangri-la ZC. There is an unfounded expectation that somehow unique intelligence can be magically imparted to the relocated individuals. If the individuals being asked to move to Shangri-la ZC do not relocate, they will not be considered again for management opportunities, a harsh but stark reality. An additional false belief is that if zip code managers are transferred to a Boondocks ZC, a miracle will happen to the Boondocks ZC team, merely by being in the presence of the Shangri-la ZC manager.

RECOMMENDATION

Forget the postage and "return to sender" the Shangri-la ZC manager. Hire only qualified, vetted individuals who exhibit the management skills you need during the interview process. You want a manager who has the capacity to interact with and groom— not talk down to—teams in the Boondocks ZC. A sense of regional pride is also likely to ensure that the Boondocks ZC teams will work harder for someone who understands the culture of the region in which they are doing business. Make sure there are at least three individuals from different reporting managers in the vetting process. There are good consulting firms fully able to identify this management style and recommend the qualified candidates regardless of their five-digit identification code.

Golf Management

Golf Management

The "golf" management style has evolved in the last forty years, and is known by several traits. A manager adhering to this style makes most (if not all) important organizational decisions somewhere between the first hole and the nineteenth—usually on the nineteenth. In the past, this management style existed primarily in male-dominated groups like zip code and elitist, thus alienating many women from corporate promotions until recently. Alcohol is involved at many levels, but not to the degree mentioned in the bar management style. Golf managers do not normally fit into the high school jock genre because most athletes view golf as a game, not a sport. The recent addition of golf sports channels has helped promote this management style and further its stature.

Golf managers focus entirely on golf; most of their buddies play golf, but don't play any other sports. There is a story that illustrates how golf-focused these individuals are, and this tunnel focus can lead to bad judgments—especially in promotion and hiring.

Ed and his three work buddies always played golf on Saturday. This particular day Ed came home a bit flushed, and his wife asked, "What's the matter?"

"It was horrible. Mark had a heart attack on the third hole."

His wife said, "That's unbelievable! What did you do?"

"Well, we played, and we dragged him. We played a bit more, and dragged him 'til we got to the last hole, then called an ambulance."

This lack of business focus can cause considerable damage to your organization because all decisions are made based on the weather and daily hole count. If one does not play golf, there is probably no chance of rising within the ranks of a company dominated by the golf management communities. Remember, the ambulance will only get called once the game is over, and by then the organizational damage may be too extensive to recover. I know of an instance in which a facility that was located in the golfing Mecca of Florida was kept open, and another facility located in a less golf-friendly climate was closed, even though the non-golf Mecca location was a better performer in every metric and had a lower cost of operation. The executives did not want to give up the perks of adding a few rounds at high-end golf resorts on the company dime to their quarterly visits.

RECOMMENDATION

Remove all such dependencies by monitoring the outings the company sponsors. Establish a senior review board that measures an individual's contributions to the company—not his *handicaps*.

Elitist Management

What do these addresses have in common?

- 341 Walnut Street, Philadelphia, PA 19104
- 116th Street and Broadway, New York, NY 10027
- 10027, Hanover, NH 03755
- Massachusetts Hall, Cambridge, MA 02138
- Day Hall Lobby, Ithaca, NY 14853

These are the addresses of some of America's most prestigious universities: University of Pennsylvania, Columbia University (New York), Dartmouth College, Harvard University, and Cornell University, respectively.

Since the inception of Harvard and other Ivy League schools, America's elite have been molded by these institutions. William Donovan scoured these places of knowledge to staff his Office of Strategic Services, the forerunner of the Central Intelligence Agency. It was a given that a degree from any of the *chosen* universities guaranteed a six-figure income. A pedigree mentality took over within America's corporations, sometimes even surpassing the old birthright societal norm that dominated the late 1800s. Once these "elitist" managers move up, they tend to hire only more silver-spoon individuals like themselves. It is suspected that this type of hiring practice may have been a course taught in the Ivy League school curriculum.

Similar to zip code management, this style of manager congregates in the Northeast and is prevalent in the once-dominated headquarters housed in the old haunts of Wall Street. American corporations in the late '80s would pay enormous salaries and stock options to the elitists only to have substandard growth over and over again. Then, if things weren't going well, elitist managers would just change to another company, and those companies would hire them no questions asked. Insanity! You know Einstein's definition of insanity: "doing the same thing over and over again expecting a different outcome." Wall Street of the mid '90s was full of elitist managers, and it wreaked havoc. This inbreeding has cost many companies substantial capital, both human and financial. Elitist managers who all hail from the same schools have the exact same training and education. They are great for maintaining a company, but cannot grow them. And as the Internet-age and computing capacity levels the competitive landscape, they do not have the gumption to stay in the game. Inevitably, as these companies who embraced elitist hiring practices plateau, they must look for talent that can move them forward. Recently, a 2010 *Bloomberg Businessweek* survey[16] showed that in the last five years, most CEO/CIO personnel no longer hailed from these schools.

Ranking	# CEOs	Undergraduate Alma Mater
1	12	University of California
2	12	School of Hard Knocks (*no undergraduate degree*)
3	11	Harvard University
4	11	University of Missouri
5	11	University of Texas
6	11	University of Wisconsin
7	10	Dartmouth College
8	9	Princeton University
9	8	Indiana University
10	8	Purdue University

RECOMMENDATION

The company must develop a solid interview and hiring regimen (regardless of university or upbringing) that allows for no exceptions, and senior management must hold firm to these guidelines. Education is important, but a solid education can be attained at universities outside of the Ivy League, and nothing beats the school of hard knocks for showing tangible capabilities.

Bar Management

Bar Management

"Bar" management has ties to several management styles, but the two closest ones are golf and zip code. I have been on several vendor sponsored golf events, and I naively assumed it was about the game. It seems that for some people in management, it's about the nineteenth hole; and I thought golf only had eighteen. I am not saying that all managers focus on the nineteenth hole, only those whose focus is the alcohol. Zip code management's relationship with business stems from the early colonial American businesses, where the business activities and decisions were done down at the local pub, or at "gentleman's clubs," and nothing was thought of it at the time. Later, as alcohol became an acceptable business write-off, bar management was firmly established in corporate America. There are some responsible managers who can properly handle themselves at the local bar gatherings—we are not addressing you, but rather your counterparts.

A bar manager needs to consume his portion of liquid courage before he can "effectively" begin the day or night, and he does so at the bar. This manager needs people to attend those after-work functions, where he can let everyone know he is in charge. A bar manager delivers his message either in veiled or direct threats, depending upon the level of liquid courage he has consumed. Invites go out to known mouthpieces to ensure his directives get back to the intended party, who is usually not present. Using surrogates means the bar manager doesn't actually have to confront the individual face-to-face.

Decisions and commitments are made that probably would not have been if bar managers had waited until they were not alcohol impaired. Many mornings are spent lamenting statements said in a liquid-courage fog that exceeded legal alcohol limits. If you are not part of this whiskey-stained veneer, you probably will miss out on most promotions. Additionally, organizational adjustments sketched out on a cocktail napkin that usually develop by the fifth drink will not include your name. Bar management may be compared to one's decision to get behind the wheel of a car after consuming more than the legal limit. It is risky, shows poor judgment, and comes with fatal consequences.

RECOMMENDATION

Senior management must be aware of these managers and move them into counseling, or move them out. A review of expense reports can help the company identify these individuals quickly so that help may be made available if they are so inclined to accept it. If not, Human Resources must step in to remove the manager.

Group No. 3

Management Styles

CONSENSUS

SALESMAN

WALL STREET

BOBBLE HEAD

GROUP OUTCOMES

- Management by Committee
- Avoids Accountability & Obfuscates
- Ignores True Opportunity Costs
- Decisions Are Not Fact-Based

Consensus Management

"Consensus" management is a well-liked style, but does nothing to advance a company. In fact, it usually relegates a company to the condition of status quo to the dismay of stockholders. This management style is designed to prevent "blame storming,"[17] and to equally share failures across the board. The good news is that meetings and committees are plentiful, allowing everyone to "contribute." The bad news is that this management structure will allow groups to perpetually tread water, engaging in paralysis by analysis.[18] They think through a problem so thoroughly that by the time they try to implement the solution the problem has changed in context or environment, making their solution moot. One strong individual in the group can derail even a relatively mature organization. It is very difficult to create a group in which the weight differential of the input is meritorious and not politically or personality driven, where every member of the team has the ability to voice an idea and have it judged on the value of data alone. It is difficult to overcome this type of management since it meets with the approval of the political correctness crowd. However, the longer it lingers, the greater the strangulation of corporate growth. The strategic individual contributors stop moving the company forward as they wait for the "consensus committee" to lead out with organizational ideas. This management style kills creativity, as no one is willing to step out unless she is also willing to use a considerable amount of time and personal capital. *Stagnation by summation* is an alternative label for this management style because it takes time for the committee to meet and publish their findings. Start-up companies can ill afford this management structure.

RECOMMENDATION

Identify a strong individual who thinks and communicates clearly, who has vision consistent with the organization's goals and values. and promote her to management to move the organization into a more directive style, implementing her visionary ideas. If you need multiple inputs, and a committee is the best way to gather this data, make sure you have a group leader (conductor) who understands how to solicit information from members who might be reticent, and set boundaries for the conversation of those that are verbose. You want a strong conductor who will tone down the shrilling of the flutes and enhance the timber of the oboe. Remember most senior managers want one throat to choke.

Salesman Management

This management style is usually short on substance and long on marketing an idea. Without the ability to define and follow through with effective execution, a "salesman" manager is exposed when problems manifest and he lacks the ability to deliver. He tends to be a cheerleader for the team, always organizing pep rallies, masquerading at motivational conferences, or bringing in someone to "reach one's inner self'" to make team members feel good. As time wears on, people will become disillusioned as they realize what they have bought into is not necessarily fulfilling. Having prettier and louder cheerleaders does not make the team on the field play a better game. In order for that to happen you need a strong coach and a talented squad.

The best way to describe this sentiment is the feeling you get on the third day after you purchase a timeshare that you neither wanted nor can afford. The euphoria (while you're at the timeshare) is matched only by the desperation you feel until you unload it.

RECOMMENDATION

The skill sets needed to sell an idea are very different from those needed to execute that idea. Put Salesmen in sales where they belong, and recruit leaders and coaches into positions where team development and performance count.

Wall Street Management

Ask one hundred college-bound students what a slide rule is, and maybe five can give you the correct answer. NASA put astronauts into space, landed them on the moon, and brought them safely home with nothing more than a simple wooden slide rule. Was the slide rule accurate? Were people willing to risk their lives on these wooden calculators? NASA treasured human capital and made sure they were exact in all of their calculations. There are managers who concentrate on precision; they care about the stark black numbers below the bottom line and have no regard for the red-blooded human capital that contributed to that figure.

In the '90s, the government changed the way a company could count earnings, and the entrepreneurs were off to the races. The managerial focus became budget-oriented and resource- myopic. The intent was not to sustain a company, but to make the company ready for sale. The government's failure to control this nonsense accounting (all in the name of job creation) has led to significant damage to new managers. These managers learned traits that were toxic.

Today these folks preach year in and year out how they can reduce the company's costs up to 25 percent, while increasing productivity by up to 10 percent, or sometimes even higher. They are praised by senior management for adding to the company's bottom line. The reality is that unless you are planning on selling the company, these managers will destroy your real capital—the individual contributors (human capital). A "Wall Street" manager usually gets fat bonuses, and promotions ensue, driving resentment deeper. A very serious pattern develops among even your better managers if you are not aware of the Wall Street manager. This thought process is easily identified; if he is over budget, he simply cuts resources (usually contractors) despite the workload in front of them. The full-time employees (FTEs) feel the brunt of having to work large amounts of uncompensated overtime. This resentment by the FTEs will eventually spill over into performance and loss of productivity. The FTEs are thinking, *surely senior management will come to their senses soon, right?* However, all too often, senior management is consumed by its own issues and blissfully ignores the resentment occurring below it.

The financial managers that are corporate bean counters are doubly deleterious to a company because they never get their noses out of a ledger long enough to see the impact of their budget cuts on the entity they are responsible for evaluating and supporting.

I remember a corporate VP of operations who had risen to his position by cutting millions of dollars from maintenance budgets. In two years he had hard bottom-line cost reductions; in five years (after he was made VP) he had three plants that had multi-million dollar pieces of equipment that were falling apart because they had been repaired with duct tape. Now the equipment issues were the plants' problem, and he could rail at them for not meeting production demands due to equipment failures.

Wall Street managers are generally shortsighted, only seeing as far as their next promotion. They are a dangerous creature to have in your organization because they only understand existing currency, not future value.

RECOMMENDATION

Be wary of purchasing a company whose main managerial thrust has been financial management, as it can become an albatross around your neck. Senior management must identify and remedy the situation either through training or dismissal. When making cost saving a key process indicator or bonus incentive, make sure that the managers understand that cost cutting should not impact product quality or long-term efficacy of the company. Senior management must be diligent when pursuing expense reductions. If a middle manager promises numbers that seem unreal, they likely are!

If finding an objective and unbiased appraisal is too difficult or politically painful in your company, perhaps the assessment of an expert outside consultant or your firm's audit partner can be helpful.

Bobble Head Management

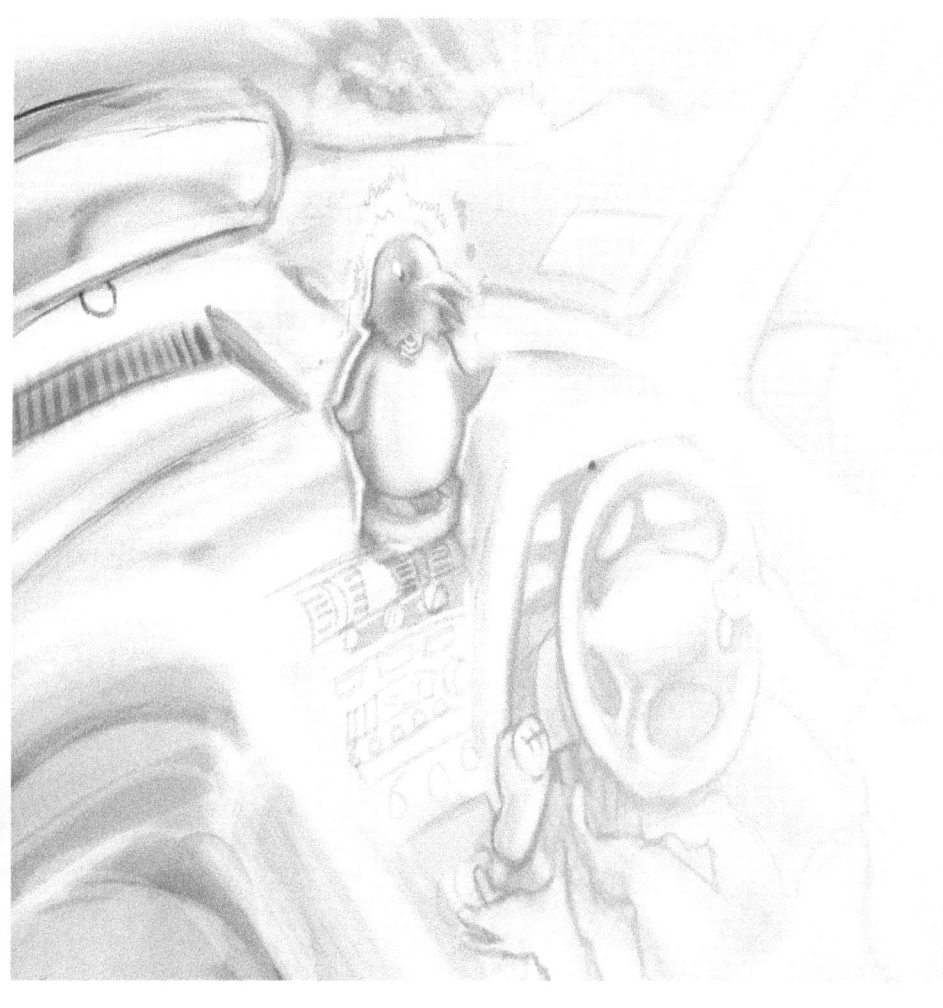

Bobble Head Management

Those of you, who grew up in the '60s, may remember seeing cars pass you on the highway with a little dog's head on the dashboard, his head bobbing up and down as if to say, "Yes, we are passing you." As cute and harmless as this may seem, "bobble head" management style is a costly one. When every statement is approved without reservation, critical information may come too late in the decision process, as no one is willing to speak up and say no. Bobble head managers look for individuals who always say yes to their ideas and decisions, promoting a deterministic environment that has fatal consequences.

Many young, talented, would-be leaders exposed to this style take one of two positions: the smart ones quietly realize it's a dead-end area and either leave the company outright or transfer to another department to work for an individual they respect and from whom they want to learn the correct skills to move upward. The other alternative is they learn to become "firefighters," trying to accomplish what their manager so foolishly has committed them to do. These individuals will eventually wear out under the constant barrage of bad decisions and usually end up leaving the company anyway. If you realize that you have a bobble head manager in your midst, you will need to learn to prod them to listen to their subject matter experts (SMEs) and be willing to say no, and offer up alternatives that are reasonable and sound.

RECOMMENDATION

The solution to exterminating a bobble head manager is for senior management to promote the idea of communication downward through the organization, stressing the importance of speaking up to present ideas, options, and alternatives.

Group No. 4

Management Styles

VISA

AFFIRMATIVE ACTION

CORPORATE NEPOTISM

POST TURTLE

GROUP OUTCOMES

- Temp Strategies Morph Into Entitlement Programs
- Incompetency & Cluelessness

Visa Management

In the late '80s, America's corporate information technology business units moved to an outsourcing model that is still present today. This caused an influx of individuals from other continents into corporate America. At the same time, growth of a cultural diversity movement and the Politically Correct were pressuring American corporations to reflect the full makeup of its workforce in their management structures.

While corporations rushed to promote cultural diversity, they were also trying to avoid being criticized by the Politically Correct, so many of them promoted candidates whether or not they were qualified. This history does not mean that there are or were no qualified individuals in management today who first came to the United States on a visa; it just means they may be viewed with certain skepticism. There are also difficulties associated with people of different ethnic origins managing other nationalities in general, and a foreign national trying to govern a U.S.-based team may very well experience this friction. This is especially true if there is a perception that the promotion was not meritorious. A general lack of respect for the visa manager can be expected, as well as labels of "inferior" and "not qualified."

RECOMMENDATION

Successful corporations will recognize the folly of the past, and will invest money and time to ensure individuals are prepared to tackle their new roles. A strong involvement from Human Resources will also help smooth the transition. Remember: many of these managers have been in the United States for quite some time, and are qualified, experienced, and have the skills that warrant their promotion to manager. Promote such individuals from within the organizations where they are assigned to aid in the overall perception of visa management as something that can be successful within your organization.

Affirmative Action Management

For the better part of the '70s and '80s, affirmative action was used to fight the heavily entrenched racism that was prevalent in management, especially in the South. "Affirmative action" management was initially needed to force the equitable change to happen. There are many instances and stories showing the success of qualified individuals, but in some situations, marginally qualified individuals were thrown into the fray with insufficient training or help. The loss of middle management during this same period only made matters worse.

This sink-or-swim mentality usually caused severe friction between employees and their new manager, sometimes escalating into lengthy legal discourse. Corporations finally pitched in and helped, but not before the damage had been done. Today this management style still exists in municipalities, school districts, and where the political correctness "minders" still have some authority. At the turn of the new century, several universities stopped using Affirmative Action as a measuring process for admissions, as yet another indication that this type of appointment was not necessary for the future.

RECOMMENDATION

If Affirmative Action management still exists at your company, discuss it with your HR team. If your company has an ethics hotline, consider reporting it there

Corporate Nepotism

Nepotism usually applies to family members who get hired by other family members instead of hiring most qualified individuals. In some firms, sons and daughters are hired and allowed to "grow up" within the organization. There is an inherent danger in hiring unqualified family members; it places an organization at great risk. In the reference I am applying within this book as it relates to a corporation, I will define nepotism a bit differently. When a corporation grows so fast that the staff is overwhelmed to the extent that normal interviewing techniques and processes go out the window, the result is "corporate nepotism." Managers tend to hire their friends or friends of friends. Qualifications are not considered, and these organizations soon find themselves over their heads. Even if an outside consulting firm is brought in for advice, it takes several corrective action iterations, some more costly than others, before changes occur. Bitterness sets in as necessary changes are implemented. Most companies stagnate and do not achieve the performance level once envisioned. These corporations will never achieve any level of cohesiveness until the old guard is completely vanquished.

RECOMMENDATION

At the outset of growth, hire a management firm or individual that specializes in organizational development to mature your organization correctly. If you are already at your desired level of growth described above, and feel you have been a victim of this management style, hire an outside firm to reorganize as quickly as possible to mitigate long-term effects of *nepotism*.

Post Turtle Management

"Post turtle" management is prevalent in most midsized companies and ballooned during the '80s due to strong economic growth. It can be seen sporadically in the larger companies but is easily identified by the best managers and therefore often eliminated. Post turtle management arises when an individual is unqualified for his job, but has an ally in senior management preventing his demise. This manager stays hidden in pockets or silos spread throughout the company and will prevent growth in those areas.

A couple of signs that will identify this management style in your organization. When your quality people start leaving the company or begin to transfer within the company to avoid the malaise created, it may be due to a Post Turtle manager. Post turtle managers often prevent promotion of qualified individuals for fear of their standing out and getting the attention. They may take action to ensure the subordinate is given mundane tasks or minor projects, keeping talent squelched. These managers surround themselves with weak subordinates in hopes senior management will mistake the Post Turtle for the source of talent and innovation and are, therefore, irreplaceable. Their fear consumes the majority of their time, allowing no time for development of their staff or the advancement of their team.

These managers hold lengthy meetings to discuss presentations, wasting subordinates' time when a simple, off-line review in advance of scheduling a team review would make these meetings productive. Post turtle managers can't seem to assimilate information into cognitive output without repeating it in a room full of people. They must feed on the talent and ideas of their team so they can regurgitate later when with their bosses.

Post turtle management might be described as an incompetent third-world dictatorship with an army just big enough to keep subordinates in line, but not large enough to do much damage to the organization. If post turtle managers get promoted, a lack of respect for senior management begins to creep into the DNA of the organization, undermining the effectiveness of management everywhere. Growth will certainly slow down, if not stop altogether. Quite possibly (and more probably), an exodus of quality people becomes inevitable.

By now you might be wondering: just what *is* a post turtle? I'll tell a story:

> While suturing up a cut on a seventy-five- year-old rancher whose hand had been caught in the gate while working his cattle, the doctor struck up a conversation. Eventually the topic got around to management.
>
> The old rancher said, "Well, ya know, some folk are like a post turtle."
>
> Not being familiar with the term, the doctor asked, "What's a post turtle?"
>
> The old rancher said, "When you're driving down a country road and you come across a fence post with a turtle balanced on top, that's a post turtle." The old rancher saw the puzzled look on the doctor's face, so he continued to explain. "You know he didn't get up there by himself, he doesn't belong up there, he doesn't know what to do while he's up there, he sure as heck ain't goin' anywhere, and you just wonder what kind of idiot put him up there in the first place."

Post Turtle

RECOMMENDATION

Make a quick call to "C"- level[19] Intelligence Agency (CIA) to overthrow the dictator and bring in fresh, pliable, and willing individuals who can be molded to the organization's intent. If there is a void in seasoned managers, engage a third-party firm to provide the needed mentorship to ensure your business's success. Surveys done by drop boxes allow for anonymity and your people will feel safe—no electronic eavesdropping.

Group No. 5

Management Styles

OFFSHORE

MERGER

PENGUIN

GROUP OUTCOMES

- Poorly Implemented Plans
- Blame Storming
- Abdicates Accountability
- Dog-Pound Recruiting Policy
- Lemming Behavior

Offshore Management

In 1962, Ross Perot created the first outsourcing company in the United States by forming Electronic Data Systems (EDS). The original purpose was to create a company specializing in one thing—centralizing the day-to-day digital data center operations of emerging companies into one location by using the latest technology. Electronic Data Systems was successful because most of the human resources utilized by EDS were U.S. based. Pretty soon other companies picked up on the idea of moving other technology areas (like code development and quality assurance) into this same model, but not in the United States.

International Business Machines (IBM) was one of the front-runners in moving from U.S. soil to other countries—especially India. The term *offshore* soon became synonymous with these activities. I have been witness to at least three attempts to send work offshore. What I found in observing each of these attempts was: (1) the lost cost of managing the project and (2) the lost time of the assigned SME to train and reduce speed of delivery (time to market) of the product under development. As corporations realize the true costs of outsourcing to their bottom line, they are starting to look at near-shore or onshore models like "rural sourcing"[20] and having great results.

There are two types of "offshore" management that reside in companies today: (1) blame storming, and (2) purpose-driven management.

BLAME STORMING

The blame storming manager views the offshore group members as her personal scapegoats when work is not meeting expectations. She is usually surrounded by weak individuals and needs someone besides her direct reports to blame for poor work. She may have supporting data that has often shown that most offshore models are ill-conceived, poorly launched, underfunded, and are assigned expectations that are not realistic. These are the stories that have been most prevalent across corporate America for the last fifteen to twenty years. There appears to be a lot of credibility to this dour assessment, but the problem is not with the strategy – it lies with the execution of the strategy.

The problem is threefold: first, corporations often turn over the most complex work to the offshore team, not acknowledging that it took years of investment in the core team to develop the knowledge. That is precisely the work that should be retained by the home team. Second, complex, domain- knowledge can only be transferred via a Vulcan "mind meld"[21] in order to meet often preposterously short milestones for the projects considered. Third, the turnover rate of offshore companies often is higher than for the contracting company, so what knowledge gets successfully transferred is constantly being diluted. It's kind of like the old school yard game of "grapevine." Get ten to twelve folks in a room and start by telling the person on the designated storyteller's right a small paragraph of information. That person, in turn, tells the next, and so on. Then ask the last person to stand up and recite what he or she was told.

The stories don't match, do they? Try the same concept, but now add in a time zone, language, and culture differences ...and you have created a long-running soap opera.

PURPOSE-DRIVEN

The second of these management types is a "purpose-driven" offshore model. This style is well planned with one to three (at most five) goals in mind. Purpose-driven management has identified the tasks, generated a project plan, and has submitted a well-defined budget to senior management. Senior management reviews the plans, budget, and milestones before giving the green light to proceed. The purpose-driven manager and his team are intimately involved and have "skin in the game"[22] (usually bonuses tied to meeting all the goals) to assure their success. The purpose-driven manager and team members have provided the information, built training schedules, and even traveled to the remote site to assist in the hiring of the individuals on their team. This management style will best meet the corporation goals for years to come. Unfortunately, this management style is appears to be practiced in few of America's corporations today.

RECOMMENDATION

If you sense your offshore model fits the blame storming style, carefully approach senior management with a plan that meets the purpose-driven style. Be prepared to show how to move from blame storming to a purpose-driven model.

David and Goliath

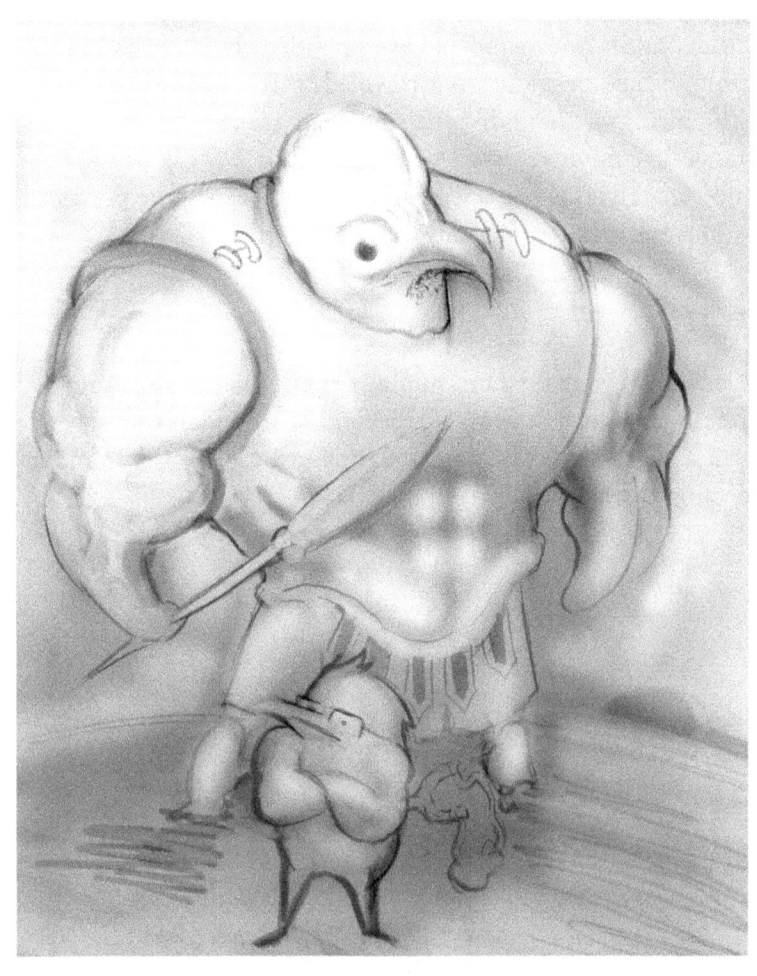

Merger Management

Merger management style evolves when a small company buys a much larger company—a David and Goliath scenario:

- The smaller company's senior management is at a loss as to how to deal with the overwhelming scale of the larger company, and spend very little time determining -which managers to keep and which managers to let go.
- The smaller company goes through several reorganization iterations, usually producing little success.

However, without an independent group analyzing who should remain or where they should end up, bad decisions are made that mostly concede to the larger company's demands. The smaller company cannot handle the larger company's decisions and overwhelming requests, and succumb to the "squeaky wheel getting the oil" syndrome. This merger management style results in unqualified people being placed into key positions.

RECOMMENDATION

Hire an outside consulting firm to assist in the formation of the newly combined organization. Consultants specializing in organizational development and governance, with experience in mergers, provide the objectivity and independence needed to avoid influence from the company's past practice, and specific expertise to be able to suggest the most effective and responsive new organization needed.

MERGER MANAGEMENT - II

This management style is an us vs. them mentality and, if not addressed early in the acquisition stage, can create dramatic organizational cleanup that sweeps out the very people you wanted to retain to run the new organization. The most prominent display of this management style is geographical in nature but can have its idiosyncrasies based on a cadre of "Type A"[23] managers. If geographical, it comes down to the North vs. South, East vs. West. Without intervention it can become a quagmire for senior management.

Senior management must assert its positive views and proactively seek out those who it wants to retain, even promoting them to the next level in advancement of the new organization. If this kind of Merger Management is based on Type A managers, then a seasoned professional is needed to help lay out the blueprint for future success. The Type A individuals whom you wish to retain need to know the true nature of the corporate line they are expected to tow, or they can create indecision that will delay or derail a company's future.

RECOMMENDATION

Encourage open communication at the lowest staff level to ensure that qualified individuals will be heard. A survey can assist such a bottom-up intervention, but only one that is truly neutral in nature and that is administered by an objective third party. The company must reach out and allow for individual contributors to voice their opinions. A senior management team should be assembled to analyze these opinions and make the appropriate decisions. In a well-executed merger, the strengths of both companies are harnessed. You create a new cultural paradigm under which both companies operate as one entity. There cannot be two playbooks.

Penguin Management

Penguins are unique creatures with unique habits, and, much like lemmings, they share one main feature: where one leads, the others follow—even it means going off a cliff. If you have ever seen lemmings falling off a cliff, you have to ask yourself why this would happen and what would cause it.

"Penguin" management shares this. These managers don't know where they are going or why they are moving in the direction they are headed, but the crowd is moving that way so it must be important. In the absence of a true leader, or any leader at all, penguin management will thrive because everyone wants to follow a leader. One day, your organization is following the one who rescued a client, the next day, someone who brings in an important new account. The only redeeming aspect of penguin management is that most of the time these new managers avoid the cliffs, and very little destruction is takes place. Quite a few start-up companies exhibit this behavior as growth occurs through acquisitions that bring in new individuals who can contribute in many different ways. Penguins latch on to new talent as if they are beacons to follow. This management style is as harmless as the namesake bird, but rarely delivers consistent growth for the organization.

RECOMMENDATION:

Hire a proven leader that will take your organization on the right path to growth. Let everyone in the organization know who the company has chosen as the leader.

Group No. 6

Management Styles

DARWIN

TESTOSTERONE

ESTROGEN

GROUP OUTCOMES

- Elitist Attitude
- Lacking Natural Ability & Talent
- Poor Road Warrior
- Martyr Syndrome

Darwin Management

Growing up I can remember parents pitting one sibling against the other with comments like, "If only you were like your older sister. She always brought home straight A's." Another memory is a parent of a close friend saying, "Your brother was able to make the team. Why couldn't you?" The parents have heard this from their parents and they turned out OK, right? Parents using this motivational factor usually end up with the opposite outcome – the child gives up.

Likewise, I heard teachers make comments to my classmates like, "I taught your brother. He never went to the principal's office." Another one said, "Your sister was a pleasure to teach. She never had any trouble with this class." These teachers never realized the permanent damage being inflicted by these thoughtless comments. Teachers using this style on students think they can change their behavior – and may. But all students observing this exchange see something different. When these students become managers they continue this learned style to control co-workers using threats (stated or implied). Their subordinates perceive these threats as real ones and, like the child, the opposite outcome is achieved – they give up.

On the first day of football practice our coaches would separate us into groups for various positions and then the fun would begin. As players would undertake their assignments playing against each other, the coach would promote the aggressive players to "motivate" the team. Certain players realized aggression would be rewarded and that winning by any means necessary soon became the norm. On Sunday afternoons across America the aggressors would be rewarded on the field (and soon worshiped) as heroes by young players who wanted to be just like them. Corporate America would become the recipient of such aggressive individuals; even though not everyone who plays football becomes a professional. Still, a majority of Americans are avid fans of the game, and its gladiators are often celebrated as iconic celebrities. As managers aggressors use what has worked for them for the better part of their lives. They pit one team of co-workers against another, never realizing the harm to co-workers or the team and the organization.

Darwin's theory postulated that humans would eventually evolve to become better and the result would be a better place to live [or work]. In each of these examples the parent, teacher and coach have a true desire for the student or sibling to become better. However, the methods which the parent, teacher and coach often use to achieve their intended outcomes will not be sustainable. The short-term effects might be achieved but the long-term outlook is debilitating. Managers who use these styles are not effective and their teams are usually low performing.

RECOMMENDATION

There is nothing wrong with encouraging internal competition amongst teams, but the net result of that competition should be the overall advancement of the company's objectives, not the glory of the team that wins.

Testosterone Management

Testosterone Management

As the name implies, this management style relates to an alpha male who typically has only male managers reporting to him. As an alpha male, the "testosterone" manager loathes a strong female leader, and often fears her—especially if she is a peer.

In this day and age, alpha males may routinely report to a female supervisor, but if so, he is not her friend. The alpha male will tolerate her for political reasons, but will not support her. He will actively work to undermine her authority. He will talk down to female peers, even if they are strong leaders, and in general will exhibit a very derisive management style toward women.

Intolerant and critical of women's mistakes, he is like a lion on the prowl—devouring when and where he can. In large meetings this testosterone manager will seek out the alpha male he aspires to be, making sure to sit by him and trying to become his closest buddy.

Even more ironic is that although the testosterone manager tends to be sports oriented, he is not necessarily a good player in any of the major sports. Heavy drinking with "the boys" and playing golf are indicators of a testosterone manager, since neither requires much athleticism.

RECOMMENDATION

Identification is difficult, so look at promotion patterns. Once identified, for the sake of the company, swiftly arrange for mentorship from a strong male who can help the testosterone manager understand the folly of his actions.

The Female Perspective of This Phenomenon
(Contributed by Padmavathi Min)

I have witnessed and been on the receiving end of two modes of the testosterone manager. The modes have dichotomous behavioral motivations, but culminate in the same organizational result. These modes are:

1. The Silverback Gorilla
2. The Cootie Boy

The Silverback Gorilla

I'm a silverback gorilla; all females need my protection and live to service me!

The first mode refers to men who only know how to relate to women who are subordinate to them financially and hierarchically. The "silverback gorilla" does not believe women are equal. He cannot accept a female as his peer, let alone his boss, and feels the only reason a woman would be his superior is because she is meeting some company quota for diversity. The competence of the female is not relevant, and he will go out of his way to undermine her authority; even going so far as to report her supposed failings to male superiors with whom he feels he has an "in."

The silverback gorilla feels he has camaraderie with men higher in the organization because he hunts with these guys on the weekend and gets away with telling sexist jokes in their presence. He is under the impression that these men agree with his view of women. This mentality usually arises in younger men who live in rural communities. They are a big fish in a little pond due to the fact that they make really good money working at the only "big" company in town. The women in the community may do little to dissuade his thinking if they are looking for someone to take care of them.

RECOMMENDATION

The silverback gorilla in the organization is allowed to exist because male counterparts and superiors have not felt it necessary to deter his behavior. He has relationships outside of work with male bosses who make him think he can get away with it. It will take another male with importance letting the gorilla know that his personal views of women have no merit in this workplace to cause a change in behavior. If diversity is important to your workforce, you will have to let the silverback go in order to prevent his vitriolic views from bleeding into the organization.

The Cootie Boy
EWEEE! You're a girl. Don't touch me. I'll get cooties!

This second mode refers to men who do not know what do with women in their organization. They are leery of women who are their peers and superiors. They do not hate women; they just cannot relate to a woman outside of the structures of mother, sister, daughter, or wife.

"Cootie boy" managers do not have any female friends. A female peer who is outgoing and aggressively business oriented is outside of their scope of knowledge. They subconsciously do not promote women because working with a strong female is uncomfortable for them. They do not actively deter women or work against them: they just do nothing to work *with* them. They are men's men, and have predefined roles for the women in their lives that are intended to reinforce their perceived safety. They know how to talk to and relate to other men, so they surround themselves with other men to avoid discomfort. They do not know what they can or cannot say in front of a female coworker and are afraid to engage in an open dialogue with them. They have been steeped in the rules of political correctness and are terrified of possible harassment issues. Therefore, they avoid working with women to impede any perceived improprieties. In short, they think that working closely with a woman will lead to getting cooties.

RECOMMENDATION

The cootie boy usually has not consciously acknowledged his discomfort with strong female roles in the workforce. Coaching him can work. Ask him to view a coworker's contributions objectively instead of thinking about who they came from, and pair him with a strong female coworker to help him get feedback on the spirit of the rules outlined by harassment law, so he is not crippled by them.

Estrogen Management

Estrogen Management

Being male, I will tread lightly here, but I thought it important to speak to the "estrogen" management style. I have heard about it numerous times from respected female colleagues. I have seen this style played out many times and have tried to figure out what motivates this management mentality, but to no avail. I personally do not understand this behavioral attitude in the workplace, but if any man could understand what drives his wife he would be a millionaire (or a great leader among men).

It seems that certain women in management do not like having other women as peers, and dislike even more having women as subordinates. Territorial issues arise and complicate the female manager's normally clear directives. As a man, I can only watch and wonder about the underlying tsunami waves of emotion as they wash ashore, bringing their destructive eroding force to bear.

One female coworker explained that jealousy plays a large part in this behavior; however, jealousy is a trait found in both men and women, so I don't know what to derive from her hypothesis. The symptom that brings out this behavior is not relevant, but it is important to acknowledge the hostile work environment it creates and to address it immediately to prevent competent female coworkers leaving for greener pastures.

I have enlisted a female manager to give me her view of estrogen management.

The Female Perspective of Estrogen Management
(Contributed by Padmavathi Min)

It has been my experience that there are three predominant modes of corrosive estrogen management. These modes are not exclusive, nor are the underlying behaviors that motivate them. These modes are:

1. The Ovary Deficient
2. The Prom Queen
3. The Bully

The Ovary Deficient

I gave up my ovaries for a seat at this board table!

The first mode refers to women who are currently in their mid-forties or older, working in industries that were, and in some cases still are, male dominated. They gave up *everything,* including their chance to have children, to be in positions of power. Their ambition and drive were detrimental to their families, and they have few if any friends of either sex. They want nothing to do with a female peer, much less a subordinate, particularly if she is younger and did not have to claw her way to the top. These women are usually at the top of their game and will continue to place the needs of the company before everything else; however, their bitterness over the sacrifices they had to make prevents them from wanting to share a seat at the table with someone they believe was given a free ride on the wagon they used to blaze a trail.

RECOMMENDATION

The willingness of the "ovary deficient" manager to do whatever it takes to meet the needs of the company is a quality that is nice to have in an organization. If you can groom younger female subordinates by defining a metric that is tied to their bonus, ovary deficient managers will likely find a way to meet that metric. The company will need to make sure there is a life/work balance.

The Prom Queen
I'm finally the queen of the prom, and all the boys adore me!

The second mode refers to the girl who was never the prom queen; she most likely did not have a sparkling personality or stunning beauty. She was average in appearance and average in popularity, but she was smart and worked hard. These women, because of the industries they work in, are surrounded by men, and being one of the few women means they get a lot of attention from men seeking their opinions and helping promote their ideas because of their "diverse" perspective. Validation from men is still the much sought after trophy, whether it is for beauty or intelligence.

It's hard for "prom queen" managers to share the limelight. They believe having other women around dilutes the attention they will get and diminishes the value of their unique female perspective.

RECOMMENDATION

The prom queen manager can be coached. She needs to be made aware of the fact that her unique contribution is appreciated outside of it being a female perspective. Sadly, the coaching will most likely have to come from a male superior.

The Bully
I'm a bully, and I keep getting promoted!

The third mode refers to women who usually know their business and use that knowledge to publicly denigrate other women's competency. They are bullies for the same reasons men are bullies—pure, raw insecurity. They target younger women who are in subordinate roles because they believe women will not fight back. They are used to working in brutish male environments. Since they cannot lash out at their male peers, who are usually the cause of their defensiveness, they target those whom they feel they have hierarchical or intellectual dominance over. This bullying behavior need not only apply to other women, but younger men in the company as well. They keep up their bullying because it has led to successful promotions.

RECOMMENDATION

The "bully" manager exists because the overall culture of the organization promotes aggressiveness. The culture of the whole organization, or subset of the organization, should be examined to determine if it is the environment that is leading to the bullying behavior. In some industries, brutish, aggressive behavior is an asset. If your industry is not one of them, or you are trying to create a less hostile work environment, this person should be removed from the organization.

Group No. 7

Management Styles

MILITARY

ENEMY AT THE GATES

DEMAND vs. RESPECT

GOOD TO GREAT

GROUP OUTCOMES

- Good Operational HARD Skills
- Lacks Innovative SOFT Skills
- Inspirational Thought Leaders
- Effective Mentors

Military Management

After World War II many individuals left the military to enter corporate America, and did a fairly decent job. However, the generals and colonels stayed in to fight the new Cold War enemy—Communism. These people later left the military to sit on corporate boards like General Electric, and provided a disciplined insight to manage disparate interests. Most lifelong military men had fathers who also were in the military, and that tends to breed a certain kind of manager. These folks are often disciplined to the point of being overbearing and are penalty-focused, especially toward creativity. "Military" management is fine in an operations area, but to move an organization forward you need that spark of ingenuity or vision.

Military managers tend to make their teams fit a strict standard by taking away individuality. They are very process-focused, thinking that tactics can solve any problem—just like in wartime conditions. This type of management is regimented to the point that by the time senior management realizes the structure in place cannot succeed, it's too late, and corporations are forced to spend considerable time and resources rebuilding their capabilities.

Also these generals and colonels have been greatly affected by the political correctness police. They were molded in the media arena to be more politicians than managers, although there are exceptions like Norman Schwarzkopf and Colin Powell.

RECOMMENDATON

Adopt a much more regimented (no pun intended) approach to promoting individual thought, and to holding each team accountable for bringing forward new ideas each year. Remember, if it comes from the top, the military man will always follow orders.

Enemy at the Gates Management

Enemy At The Gates Management

*E*nemy at the Gates is an interesting movie, especially in the beginning where it enlightens the public about which resources are considered important to the Russian government (management) and which are not. If you have seen the movie, this will be a repeat of the opening scene.

Jude Law portrays the main character, a peasant, who is conscripted in Moscow to fight the Germans as the last line of defense in Stalingrad. He is not given a gun because there was a shortage of equipment (tools to do his work). However, Jude is told to follow a fellow armed soldier, and when that soldier dies, Law's character can pick up the gun and continue the fight. (The scene can be a metaphor for resentment of fellow coworkers who get the guns while others don't.) As Law's character heads into battle, he has to decide whether to press forward against overwhelming odds or retreat, because the numbers fighting against him are staggering (all of the project work). If he retreats, his own countrymen (i.e., management) will open fire. Very few people survive long in this theater of operations.

The idea presented is one in which there are limited resources (the guns and bullets), but an ample supply of "replaceable" human capital. It is presumed that, due to the plethora of supply, the human capital can be exploited with no cost. Now translate that into a managerial style where you do not give the proper tools for success to your employees and you consider the human capital to be expendable. "Enemy at the Gates" management wears out the Human Resources department because this management style maintains that it can easily replenish these resources with people desperate for a job at any cost and generally at lower pay. (Does outsourcing come to mind?) The atmosphere is one of limited hope and a confinement to a life of drudgery.

This management style challenges the most experienced senior management structure, because it revels in the alarming body count. Enemy at the Gates managers explain away the need to worry about experienced people (SMEs) leaving, whom they believe to be an expendable group of folks who could not cut it, or those who did not align with the new management style, even though the SMEs' opinions have previously been the foundation upon which the company had stood, prospered, and grown. There are times when new direction and new blood is needed, but change needs to be measured, and then applied.

RECOMMENDATION

Place these managers directly in the cross-hairs and fire—I mean literally fire. Senior management must recognize the attrition rate, and then determine immediately where the cause lies by reaching out to those who have left and getting the specific information to correct the situation. For every year a valuable employee has been with the company, the corporate knowledge lost when they leave can't be measured, but will be felt.

Don't throw the baby out with the bath water. There are times in the corporate life cycle when reorganization and restructuring need to occur in order to ameliorate a company to the new competitive environment. But by letting go of all you SMEs, you lose all of the tacit knowledge in your organization. Your company will spend a lot of time reinventing the wheel because you allowed the folks that know the mechanics of your company to get shot in the initial exchange of volley fire. You need to spend the time to figure out which folks can be groomed for the new environment and give them a role in mentoring the next generation coming in. This harnesses their tacit knowledge and flattens the learning curve of the new troops.

Demand Vs. Respect
Management

"**D**emand" managers are a cancer to your organization. They breed a wake of destruction that results in enormous casualties. They will also set your company back several years for every year they are allowed to stay in power, at possibly a 3:1 ratio.

This type of insidious management does not care about the human toll left behind. Demand managers only care about who will succumb and conform. These people are amoral in nature, lack integrity, are deceitful in practice, and place everyone on notice to either conform or be gone. Don't confuse operating within the clique with agreement on the agenda; people have adapted to survive. The term *fearful* comes to mind, as many subordinates spend week after week jumping to the demands of management, in terror of failing. There are many examples of demand management such as:

- Canceling large meetings ten minutes before they are scheduled to start
- Rescheduling and expecting that you move your previously scheduled meetings to accommodate the demand manager's calendar
- Scheduling meetings after normal work hours

- Sending out e-mails after normal works hours with deadlines for early the next morning
- Weekend work because the manager failed to take the time to outline what was due the following week.

All of your scheduled work is pushed aside to deliver what the demand manager wants when he or she wants it, causing undue angst among his subordinates.

Out of fear, a "cover your assets" policy will ensue among subordinates, and the fear will permeate the hierarchical organization, growing like a cancer, suffocating the life out of the good cells. Each time workers go back to originally scheduled strategies, the ramp up to move the agenda forward is costly in lost time and productivity. For demand managers, the question arises daily: "Who can be walked on today to further a personal agenda?" Demand managers prepare a healthy serving of finger-pointing salad for their meetings.

RESPECT MANAGEMENT

The other type of management mentioned here is one of respect—respect for everyone at the corporation and for the corporation's clients. You can usually identify "respect" management by the following traits: (1) low employee turnover, (2) respect of peers, (3) respect of senior management, and (4) a substantial number on the leadership team will have worked together at one time or another. Respect is at the core of human interaction. People must respect each other, even when they don't necessarily agree all the time. Respect and integrity go hand in hand for these managers. There is a quote by former U.S. Senator Alan K. Simpson,[24] which goes something like this: "If you have integrity, nothing else matters; if you don't have integrity, nothing else matters." This is so true of this management style and what it demands.

The field of U.S. politics is a good example of the erosion of respect management. Early in the '80s, the United States had a president in power from one party and a Congress from another. Despite this divided government, a mutual respect for each other's ideas and a gentleman's agreement to disagree prevailed. There was not a hatred of individuals—just a philosophical difference. I am not talking about compromise, but rather a working respect of competing ideologies. In the early part of the '90s, the United States witnessed a trend leading to polarization and absolutes among the parties and branches of government, not common ground.

RECOMMENDATION

Identify demand management as quickly as possible, and remove it before this cancer cripples the organization. Human Resources will need to be engaged, especially if the senior management doesn't care or are so autocratic themselves or hopelessly overrun by the stress of work that they willfully ignore all of the symptoms of demand management.

Good To Great Management

Have you ever walked into a meeting and been able to identify who the strong managers were? I do not mean the most popular, nor do I mean the dominant room hogs. I am describing those managers who are solid, honest individuals who will charge the cannons for the company because of their belief in the company's mission. These managers quickly structure their organization to fit what the company's desires are, while at the same time meeting the human demands of the job. The manager's first move is to hire his replacement and go to great efforts to mentor his subordinates. He recognizes that without his replacement in place, he will be deemed irreplaceable. If you can't be replaced then you can't be promoted. These managers are quick to compliment subordinates, peers, or their current supervisors, and are always in a positive mood even when work is stressful. They feel at ease up and down the spectrum of management.

Although a lot of good companies manage to accomplish getting people on the right bus heading in the right direction, as mentioned in Jim Collins' book *Good to Great*,[25] Collins goes on to state the move to greatness is to get the right people in the right seat, heading down the right road. That means the people you want for your management team should support one another. They are people who are respected by peers and subordinates alike. But most of all, they are people who know how to treat their coworkers with dignity and respect. I am not saying that everyone has to agree with one another, but each of these managers listen and provide construc-tive feedback to their peers. These people feel comfortable talking to the A-, B- and C-level folks and treat everyone the same, regard-less of their title. It is these individuals who will carry the company forward on their shoulders; they are the bedrock, the foundation upon which greatness can be built. The reason these managers are able to accomplish all this is that they got their greatness the old-fashioned way—they earned it by asking for mentoring, feedback, and constructive senior input. These folks lay out a plan to get there; they adjust, they tweak, but most of all, they know where the company is headed and are on board. Remember, there are several words that only great leaders are able to utter: "I made a mistake," "Thank you," "I am sorry," and "How are you doing?"

Management Vs. Leadership

Can a great leader inspire? Can a single leader move a company from good to great? I only have to look at the Apple Corporation and Steve Jobs over the last ten years. Good companies tend to have several good leaders and managers, but lack a single great leader.

I worked for a start-up company during the tail end of the dot-com collapse, and Sales was trying its best to generate revenue. The usual method was to give training away, promise things the code could not do, and come back to the office with a contract that put pressure on the company to deliver what they had promised, and Development had to work over time to make good. The CEO at my start-up held a breakfast every Tuesday during which she asked for ideas and suggestions from the lowly support staff, all the way to the senior vice president of Sales and Marketing. On one such occasion, after a salesperson had promised the world and I had spent the last several weekends working to deliver the impossible, I made a suggestion to her that the next time Sales promised the world that *we* should get a share of their commissions. Of course you can imagine how the Sales folks felt about my suggestion, but I could see wheels turning in her head. Several weeks later the largest contract we had ever landed was announced, and of course that was also the time we got the news of what we had to deliver. After reading the requirements, we soon realized that we would need to put in many weekends to deliver, again, on promises made by Sales. Suffice it to say we did deliver, wrapping up late Sunday evening just prior to the deadline.

The following Monday, however, I found an envelope from the CEO on my chair. You can imagine my surprise when I read the letter acknowledging my suggestion and examined the enclosed check. She had indeed taken the commission and divided it across the affected organization, a bold move on her part. However, the move resulted in a significant shift within the Sales department. Now, before committing to anything, Sales would always check with us about contract demands from potential clients. Another unknown effect was the loyalty she garnered from all within the company.

Shortly thereafter, an installation was going badly at a client site, and the culprit was another vendor who was way behind schedule. It appeared that someone would have to work through the Christmas break. Before she could ask for volunteers, several of us got together and developed a schedule to cover the remote installation. One individual, who was also a recipient of the checks, even went with her on the day of his wedding anniversary to close the sale. The CEO allowed a server to be set up for the employees to play a popular game, and at certain times during the day, a broadcast e-mail would go out for everyone to jump on the server and play. Her ability to reach her people at the human level resulted in corporate capital not measurable on any balance sheet.

Was she a remarkable individual? No, but what she did was earn the respect of her employees, motivating them to achieve excellence, and thus moving the company toward greatness. The start-up company was sold to a zip code type company that did not understand this style of management, and soon pigeon management was the norm.

Are great leaders born? If we use Moses' story in the Bible, the answer would be no. So what attributes make a great leader? What distinguishes a good leader from a great leader? Companies spend millions of dollars each year trying to figure this out. Is there a simple answer? Probably not, or it would have been answered long ago by the scholars. Some people believe there is a component of luck involved, but I have a definition for luck that more or less sets the stage for making the leap from an average leader to a great leader. Luck is "when preparation meets opportunity." In case opportunity only knocks once, the great leaders are always ready. Great leaders are in constant preparation mode, sponges willing to soak up information at every turn, but what separates them is they retain their humanity. I can give fifty strong candidates the same management skills training, and only two to three will rise to the top. Why is this? In this iSeries age we live in, human contact is lacking. Just look at the time our children spend with an electronic device. In the '70s the electronic age was evolving, and human relationships were greatly impacted. Some may say we are stuck in an electronic vortex.

You will find great leaders prioritize the value of human capital. They volunteer, give back to the community, and know each of their employees personally. That does not mean they are best friends forever, though. There is a difference between personal BFFs and a manager-to-subordinate relationship. A bumper sticker I love describes best-friend relationships, which are not necessarily best for a great company. The bumper sticker states, "A good friend will help you move a couch; a best friend will help you hide a body." In a company structure, you need to know where the bodies are buried, so you can bring the guilty to light and remove them, not hide them.

In the demand vs. respect section, I mention integrity. I would like to relate a story I think demonstrates both integrity and leadership. At the outset of World War II, conscientious objectors were not viewed as patriotic, and were ridiculed by most enlistees. There was an army corporal who was just such an individual, and during the combat training, the soldiers of his platoon alienated and ridiculed him. But his unyielding convictions and selfless acts of courage in saving the lives of the very men who ridiculed him won him their awe and respect. He emerged from the war as a Medal of Honor recipient. The gentleman I am referring to is Desmond Doss. Desmond's luck would place him in a situation for which he was well prepared because of his beliefs, not the army's training. The men who had ridiculed him nominated him for the Medal of Honor. You may ask yourself how that can be. The integrity he showed overwhelmed any prejudices the men had. Many of Desmond's soldiers would eventually say, "I want this guy next to me in my foxhole."

Many companies have good managers and good leaders; this is not enough. Great leaders in senior management positions of your company will move your organization from good to great. Great leaders aren't necessarily great managers. Leadership entails a unique set of skills that differ from the basic skills attributed to effective managers. However, your great leaders should always be in senior management if your company wants to move from good to great. Remember that inventories need management, but your workers need leadership. The comparative analysis of leaders vs. managers is beyond the scope of the exploration of management styles. It is an intriguing topic that I'll address in the follow-up book to *Pigeons • Penguins • Post Turtles*.

I hope this book has been informative and generated its fair share of chuckles. I leave you with a quote from Rosalynn Carter: "A leader takes people where they want to go. A great leader takes people where they don't necessarily want to go, but ought to be."

End-Notes

1. The exact origin of baseball is unknown, but most historians agree the game is based on the English game of "rounders." Rounders became popular in the United States in the early nineteenth century, and was called "town ball," or "base," which eventually became known as "baseball." Originally there were many variations of the rules, and since 1845, the debate persists about crediting either Alexander Cartwright or Abner Doubleday as the father of baseball (as it is presently known). The first professional baseball league, the National Association, was formed in 1871, and has evolved ever since until the formation of the Major League Players' Association took shape in 1953, which continues to represent players' interests today. | http://www.mlb-players.com/history.php.

2. The original quotation source is unknown, but the quotation is well-established within the U.S. English language.

3. The concept of an Internet-Year is one that emphasizes the speed at which the business cycle seems to work for Internet-oriented, eBusiness enterprises to work. One attempt to quantify that pace seems worth considering and passes the "feels right" test to this author. Eric Reiss in a blog post September 2009 suggests the pace is on the order of one Internet Year for each quarter calendar year. See www.fatdux.com/blog/.../calculating-the-length-of-an-internet-year/

4. Jim Collins, *Good to Great: Why Some Companies Make the Leap... And Others Don't.* (New York, New York – HarperCollins Publishers Inc. 2001).

5. Zhouying Jin, *Global Technological Change: From Hard Technology to Soft Technology*, Chapter 7 "Soft-Tech Talents and the Education Revolution." (city: Intellect Press, 2005 (ISBN: 1-84150-124-7), pp. 257-261. People qualified in soft technology (e.g.: management, economics, finance, statistics, price analysis, national economic planning, intelligence services, cultural/social industries) are interdisciplinary experts capable of creating new industries and institutions.

6. The iGeneration, or often referred to Generation—Z represents those born from the mid-1990s or early 2000's to the present. These are kids who have had access to the Internet and Internet appliances of various kinds their entire life. See Wikipedia for the search term Generation-Z or iGeneration.

7. Michael Day, "Hi-tech is turning us all into time-wasters," *Guardian.Co.UK / The Observer,* (July 20, 2008) http://www.guardian.co.uk/science/2008/jul/20/psychology.mobilephones.

Research by Dr. Piers Steel (Haskayne School of Business, University of Calgary) in the field of Human Resources and Organizational Dynamics indicates that the incidence of chronic procrastination has risen dramatically in recent decades, from one person in 20 to one in four, as new technology has come to dominate our lives. Even the beeps notifying the arrival of email are said to be causing 0.5 percent drop in gross domestic product (GDP) in the U.S., costing the economy $70 billion per year.

8. iPad: Apple (1 Infinite Loop, Cupertino, California 95014) was assigned the iPad trademark (USPTO Serial No. 76497338) on March 17, 2010 after acquiring the entire interest from Fujitsu Frontech North America Inc. Fugjitsu originally was awarded the

trademark in March 2003 for their wireless handheld computing device. See USPTO trademark assignment record: http://assignments.uspto.gov/assignments/q?db=tm&sno=76497338.

9. iPod, iPad, iPhone: The reference to these trademarked products within the text of this publication are used in compliance with the trademark and service mark legal list policy of Apple, Inc. http://www.apple.com/legal/trademark/appletmlist.html.

10. DROID™ and Droid™ are registered trademarks of Lucasfilm Ltd., and its related companies. On October 9, 2009, Lucasfilm Ltd., the American production company founded by *Star Wars* creator George Lucas, filed to protect the trademark DROID™ and Droid™ in relation to "wireless communications devices, including mobile phones, cellular phones, handheld devices, and personal digital assistants, accessories and parts thereof, and related computer software and wireless telecommunications programs; mobile digital electronic devices for the sending and receiving of telephone calls, electronic mail, and other digital data, for use as a digital format audio player, and for use as a handheld computer, electronic organizer, electronic notepad, and digital camera; downloadable ring tones and screen savers; cameras, pagers and calling cards" and "communication services, namely, transmission of voice, audio, visual images and data by telecommunications networks, wireless communication networks, the Internet, information services networks and data networks; wireless communications services."

11. Facebook: The Facebook reference within the text of this publication is used in compliance with the brand permissions policy of this social network service: http://www.facebook.com/brand-permissions/index.php.

12. March Madness® is protected by trademark law, and its reference within the text of this publication is not used in a commercial context to promote some other service or product. It

is used herein as a colloquial reference to the annual season-ending NCAA division basketball tournament that is familiar to the general U.S. population as an annual sporting event. The term is controlled exclusively by the holding company, "March Madness Athletic Association, LLC" (MMAA) .

13. Source: "NetLingo" The Internet Dictionary | http://www.netlingo.com/index.php.

NetLingo has thousands of definitions that explain the online world of business, technology, and communication including the largest collection of Internet acronyms and text messaging shorthand. NetLingo caters to students, teachers, parents, gamers, designers, techies, bloggers, journalists, and industry professionals worldwide.

Catherine Holahan, "Keeping Up with the Web's New Lingo," *BusinessWeek.com*, (The McGraw-Hill Companies | 4/12/2007) http://www.netlingo.com/news/Business_Week.pdf.

14. Jonathan LaPook, "Digital Distractions Affect the Bottom Line." CBS News (July 11, 2011) CBS News Video: http://www.cbsnews.com/stories/2011/07/11/eveningnews/main20078420.shtml.

15. An application-sharing and conferencing service that is widely used for presentations, demonstrations, training, and support from WebEx Communications, Inc., Santa Clara, CA (www.webex.com). Everything that the presenters see and manipulate on their computers can be viewed by everyone in the conference. WebEx uses either an ActiveX control or Java applet in the computer at each end of the conference, and installation for new attendees is automatic. Meetings can be set up instantly or scheduled, and voice is handled by voice over IP (VoIP) or traditional PSTN conference calling. Founded in 1996, the company became a wholly owned subsidiary of Cisco in 2007.

16. James E. Ellis, "Top 10 CEO Undergraduate Alma Maters," *Bloomberg Businessweek*, May 13, 2010. http://www.businessweek.com/magazine/content/10_21/b4179020050124.htm. The Bloomberg ranking of CEO undergraduate alma maters shows corporate chieftains come from across the country.

> Where CEOs at America's Largest Companies Went to College http://www.usnews.com/education/best-graduate-schools/top-business-schools/mba-jobs/articles/2010/11/15/where-ceos-at-americas-largest-companies-went-to-college

17. Blame storming: A meeting intended to determine why a deadline was missed or a project failed, and who was responsible (e.g., identifying a scapegoat) | http://www.urbandictionary.com/define.php?term=Blamestorming

18. Paralysis by Analysis: This phrase describes a situation where the opportunity cost of decision analysis exceeds the benefits that could be gained by enacting some decision. The basic idea has been expressed through narrative from a number of sources throughout history:

> William Shakespeare's *The Tragedy of Hamlet, Prince of Denmark* (written between 1599 and 1601), the main character, Prince Hamlet, is often said to have a mortal flaw of thinking too much, such that his youth and vital energy are "sicklied o'er with the pale cast of thought."

> Mrs. Edmund Craster, *Cassell's Weekly Magazine* (an untitled? poem published therein, circa (the magazine or the poem is from 1871?)1871), "The centipede was happy, quite until the toad in fun said, 'Pray, which leg goes after which?'/And worked her mind to such a pitch, she lay distracted in the ditch—considering how to run."

19. C-Level: refers to senior executives with "Chief" titles (e.g., Chief Executive Officer (CEO), Chief Operating Officer (COO),

Chief Information Officer (CIO), Chief Technology Officer (CTO), etc.)

20. Jennifer Alsever, "Forget India, Outsource to Arkansas" CNN|Money (July 8, 2010). http://money.cnn.com/2010/07/08/smallbusiness/rural_onshoring/index.htm. Rural sourcing: Dubbed "rural sourcing," "rural outsourcing," and "onshoring," the practice relies on two simple premises: smaller towns need jobs, and they offer a cheaper cost of living than urban centers. Businesses that outsource work to these areas can expect to pay less—rates are often as much as 25 percent to 50 percent lower than if they were hiring urbanites with comparable skills.

21. Vulcan: A character from the 1964 American science fiction entertainment franchise *Star Trek* created by Gene Roddenberry. Vulcans (or sometimes "Vulcanians") are an extraterrestrial humanoid species noted for their attempt to live by reason and logic, with no interference from emotion. According to the story, many Vulcans are contact telepaths. The "mind meld" is a subset of the Vulcan telepathic abilities for sharing thoughts, experiences, memories, and knowledge with another humanoid.

22. Skin in the Game: A phrase that has been traced as far back as early twentieth century U.S. newspaper articles, and its use traced to many continents, including Australia. The phrase is often attributed to Warren Buffet, but he does not claim credit for originating the phrase. The skin in this case is a synecdoche (a figure of speech) for the self, much as "head" stands for cattle and "sail" for ships. The game is the investment, commitment, or gamble being undertaken. Thus, investors in a company will be more comfortable in their own skins if they know that the managers are personally invested as well, that is, they share the risk and have an incentive to share the gains.

   William Safire, "Language: Who's got a skin in the game?—Editorials & Commentary—International Herald Tribune,"

New York Times, http://www.nytimes.com/2006/09/17/
opinion/17iht-edsafire.2839605.html.

23. Meyer Friedman, *Type A Behavior: Its Diagnosis and Treatment*,
(city: Kluwer Academic Press, 1996), p. 31. The Type-A and
Type-B personality theory (also known as the Jacob Goldsmith
theory) was originally published in the 1950s. The theory describes two common and contrasting personality types: Type
A (high-strung) and Type B (easygoing). Type-A: The theory
describes this individual as a "workaholic"—ambitious, aggressive, businesslike, controlling, highly competitive, impatient,
preoccupied with his or her status, time-conscious, and tightly
wound.

24. U.S. Senator (1979–1997). "Biographical Directory of the
United States Congress (1774–Present)." http://bioguide.con-
gress.gov/scripts/biodisplay.pl?index=s000429

25. Jim Collins, *Good to Great: Why Some Companies Make the Leap...
And Others Don't,* (city: Greenwich Publishing Group, 1997)